Donuts in Love

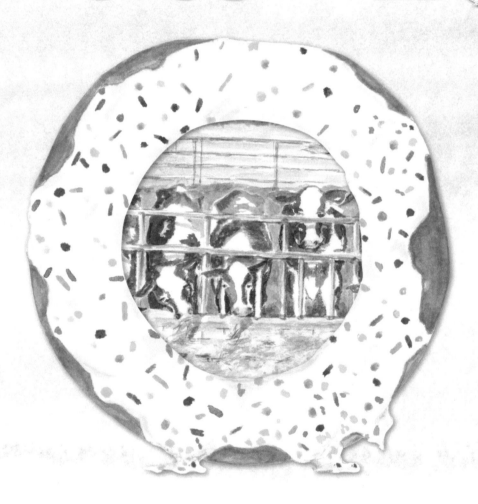

Shelley Vieira

Illustrated by Maggui Ledbetter

Whether you are a Nono or a Vovo,
may your grandchildren feel loved
and always remember you.

In memory of Manuel Vieira (Vovo)
and
Mario DeFrancesco (Nono)

Grandchildren are the crowning glory of the aged;
parents are the pride of their children.
(Proverbs 17:6 NLT)

"Donut forget"
Indeed, he loves
his people;
all his holy ones are
in his hands.
(Deuteronomy 33:3)

Dear Reader,

I would like to share a series of text messages sent between my niece, Heather, and me while I was working on this book. I am so thankful for the Lord's encouragement and, in the case of these messages, a sign that I was on the right track. After sending the picture below to my niece by text message, this was how our conversation went.

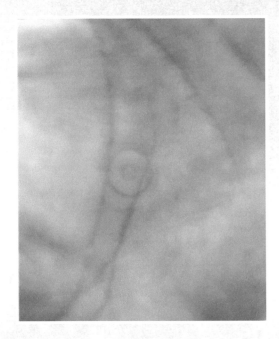

If you look close in the center of my palm, can you see something, and does it remind you of someone?

I think a circle in another circle. What is that? I don't know why but the first person that popped into my head was Vovo, but I don't know why. Who does it remind you of?

Well, you got it ◉! I was praying for God's help and direction with a book I wrote about Vovo and asking if it was okay and pleasing to him. I was working on the part where I am going to place Donuts of Love from God to us. For instance, Donut fear for I hold you by the right hand (Isaiah 41:13). As I was talking to God about it, I looked at my left hand and saw this sign. It was crazy! Crazy Good!! A God wink ;)

Holy cow, Aunt Shelley. I didn't even see that until you said that, but for some reason, the second I saw it, I thought of Vovo. I'm telling you, things like that get me all emotional! Happy tears! There's no doubt God gave you your answer. That's so amazing. I can't wait to read that book.🖤

That is so amazing that, for some reason, you thought of Vovo.Love you Heather!🖤

Love you, Aunt Shelley!!🖤

Once upon a time,
and it seems like yesterday,
four families lived on dairies,
and the cows stood eating hay.

7

Heigh-ho, Heigh-ho.
Left Rollen Donuts.
Now he'll go
to see his pride and joys.
Oh what love.
Heigh-ho, Heigh-ho,
Heigh-ho, Heigh-ho.

El Nido 11
Los Banos 34
Gilroy 82

CALIFORNIA
59
SOUTH

MERCED
California
7N90455
RAZZARTO

9

Bright and early,
Saturday mornings would arrive,
knock, knock, knock,
and the kids would come alive.

Nothing better than
to see his big grin,
holding the pink box
with yummy donuts tucked within.

"Don't take just one,
have a few.
I brought plenty!"
said their Vovo.

Then hugs and sugary kisses,
as they said their goodbyes.
Hurry close the door;
don't let in the flies!

Knock, knock, knock,
house number two,
"Are you awake yet?
I've got donuts for you."

They all gathered round
to gaze in the box.
"Vovo you're so awesome,
yes, you rock!"

How he loved to see the excitement the donuts brought,
but true happiness
was in the time that they got.

Setting off
back to the home ranch
where the boys waited,
now was their big chance.

"Get the milk,
grab a glass!
Slow down boys,
you're growing too fast!"

Surrounded once again
by those he loved the most.
Blessed by the donuts
that brought them so close.

Heigh-ho, Heigh-ho,
"Hello Steve, hurry up, go slow!
It's time for him to
go and rest."
Heigh-ho, Heigh-ho,
Heigh-ho, Heigh-ho.

Reclining in his chair,
"Oh, what a day.
Lord, thank you for my family
and the cows that eat the hay."

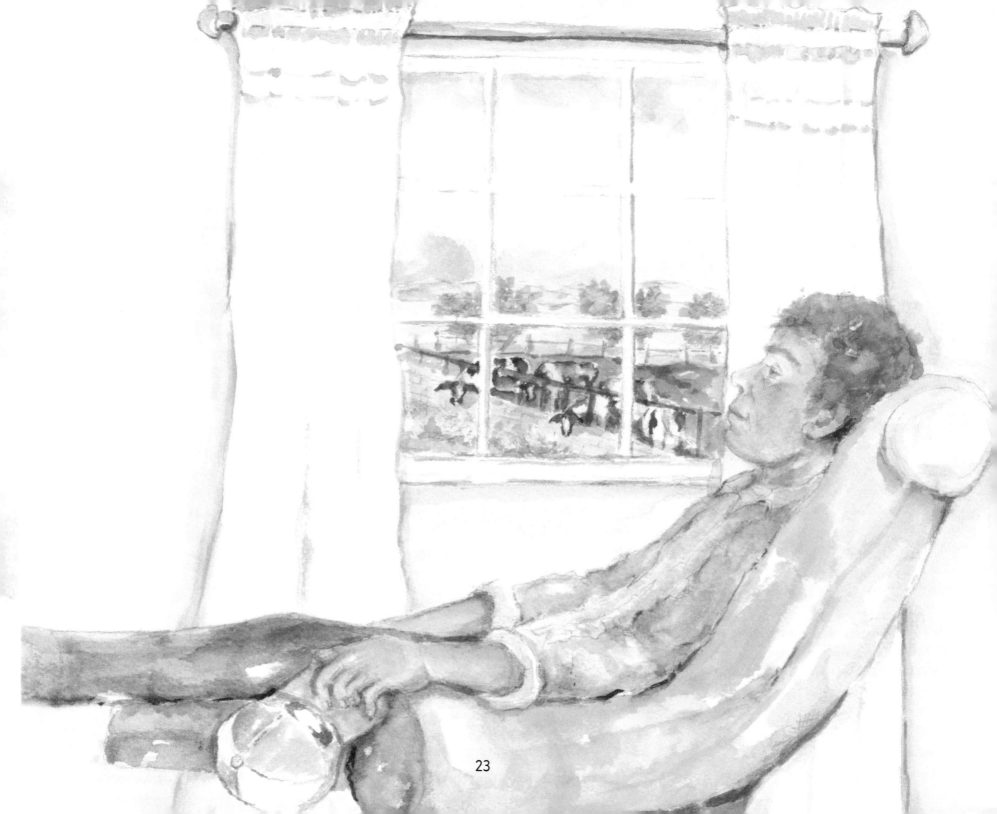

Now heaven has Vovo,
and the Father's house has many doors.
I can't wait to hear
knock, knock, knock once more.

Donuts in Love from ABOVE

Wait!
Can you hear another knock?
At your heart's door,
it's the Lord our Rock.
He gives donuts in love
just like Vovo.
Taste and see.
Yes, have a few!
Let them fill you up,
safely tucked away.
They will see you through
dark or shiny days.

"Donut forget"
Taste and see
the Lord is good;
Blessed is the man who
takes refuge in him.
(Psalm 34:8)

Donuts in Love from Above

1. **Donut forget how much I love you!**

   For God loved the world so much that he gave his one and only Son, so that everyone who believes in him will not perish but have eternal life. (John 3:16 NLT)

   See how very much our Father loves us, for he calls us his children, and that is what we are! (1 John 3:1 NLT)

2. **Donut forget you are strong!**

   God is our refuge and strength, always ready to help in times of trouble. (Psalm 46:1 NLT)

   A final word: Be strong in the Lord and in his mighty power. Put on all of God's armor so that you will be able to stand firm against the strategies of the devil. (Ephesians 6:10–11 NLT)

   For I can do everything through Christ who gives me strength. (Philippians 4:13 NLT)

3. **Donut forget to sing and praise!**

   I will sing to the Lord because he has been good to me. (Psalm 13:6)

   I will praise you, Lord, with all my heart; I will tell of all the marvelous things you have done. I will be filled with joy because of you. I will sing praises to your name, O Most High. (Psalm 9:1–2 NLT)

4. **Donut forget My mercy!**

   The faithful love of the Lord never ends! His mercies never cease. Great is his faithfulness; his mercies begin afresh each morning. (Lamentations 3:22–23 NLT)

   Answer my prayers, O Lord, for your unfailing love is wonderful. Take care of me, for your mercy is so plentiful. (Psalm 69:16 NLT)

5. **Donut forget to be thankful.**

   It is good to give thanks to the Lord, to sing praises to the Most High. It is good to proclaim your unfailing love in the morning, your faithfulness in the evening (Psalm 92:1–2 NLT)

   Always be joyful. Never stop praying. Be thankful in all circumstances, for this is God's will for you who belong to Christ Jesus. (1 Thessalonians 5:16–18 NLT)

6. **Donut forget you're protected!**

   He will cover you with his feathers. He will shelter you with his wings. His faithful promises are your armor and protection. (Psalm 91:4 NLT)

   For the angel of the Lord is a guard; he surrounds and defends all who fear him. (Psalm 34:7 NLT)

   Guard me as you would guard your own eyes. Hide me in the shadow of your wings. (Psalm 17:8 NLT)

7. **Donut limit Me!**

   Now all glory to God, who is able, through his mighty power at work within us, to accomplish infinitely more than we might ask or think. (Ephesians 3:20 NLT)

   For nothing is impossible with God. (Luke 1:37 NLT)

   Come and see what our God has done, what awesome miracles he performs for people. (Psalm 66:5 NLT)

8. **Donut fear!**

   Don't be afraid, for I am with you. Don't be discouraged, for I am your God. I will strengthen you and help you. I will hold you up with my victorious right hand. (Isaiah 41:10 NLT)

   The Lord is my helper, so I will have no fear. What can mere people do to me? (Hebrews 13:6 NLT)

9. **Donut forget to listen to My voice!**

   My sheep listen to my voice, I know them, and they follow me.(John 10:27 NLT)

   My heart has heard you say, "Come and talk with me." And my heart responds, "Lord I am coming." (Psalm 27:8 NLT)

10. Donut forget to forgive.

Forgive us our sins, as we have forgiven those who sin against us. If you forgive those who sin against you, your Heavenly Father will forgive you. But if you refuse to forgive others, your Father will not forgive your sins. (Mathew 6:12, 14 NLT)

But the Lord our God is merciful and forgiving, even though we have rebelled against him. (Daniel 9:9 NLT)

11. Donut forget to trust Me!

Trust in the Lord with all your heart; do not depend on your own understanding. Seek his will in all you do, and he will show you which path to take. (Proverbs 3:5–6 NLT)

See, God has come to save me. I will trust in him and not be afraid. The Lord God is my strength and my song; he has given me victory. (Isaiah 12:2 NLT)

Don't let your hearts be troubled. Trust in God, and trust also in me. (John 14:1 NLT)

12. Donut forget home!

There is more than enough room in my Father's home. If this was not so, would I have told you that I am going to prepare a place for you? When everything is ready, I will come and get you, so that you will always be with me where I am. (John 14:2–3 NLT)

For this world is not our permanent home; we are looking forward to a home yet to come. (Hebrews 13:14 NLT)

Let's have some fun.
Get a pink box
Chosen one.

Grab paper, scissors, and decor.
Make some donuts
to memorize and store.

What do you need to be reminded of?
Are you fearful?
Have you forgotten you're loved?

Scripture has power, this I know!
Take it with you.
Wherever you go.

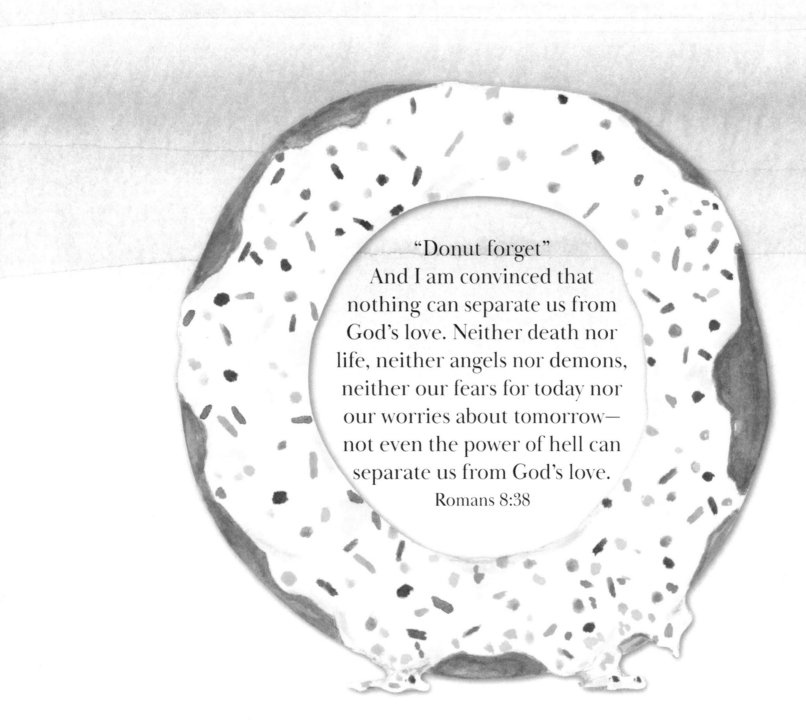

"Donut forget"

And I am convinced that nothing can separate us from God's love. Neither death nor life, neither angels nor demons, neither our fears for today nor our worries about tomorrow—not even the power of hell can separate us from God's love.

Romans 8:38

Ten More To Store

1. "You must not have any other God but me."

   (D●nut love anything more than God.)
   (Exodus 20:3)

2. "You must not make a idol of any kind and never bow and worship them."

   (D●nut make anything more important than God.)

3. "You must not misuse the name of the Lord your God."

   (D●nut forget to always say God's name with love and respect.)

4. "Remember to observe the Sabbath day by keeping it holy."

   (D●nut forget to honor God by resting on the seventh day of the week.)

5. "Honor your father and mother."

   (D●nut forget to love and respect your mom and dad.)

6. "You must not murder."

   (D●nut hurt anyone with words or action.)

7. "You must not commit adultery."

   (D●nut forget to always be faithful to your husband or wife.)

8. "You must not steal."

   (D●nut take anything that isn't yours.)

9. "You must not testify falsely against your neighbor."

   (D●nut forget to always tell the truth.)

10. "You must not covet your neighbor's house, wife, or anything that belongs to them."

    (D●nut wish for other people's things. Be happy with what you have.)

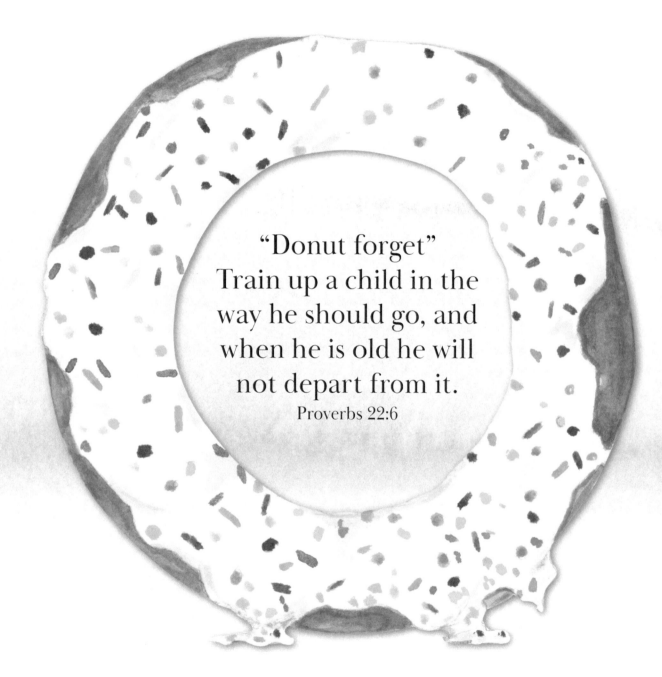

"Donut forget"
Train up a child in the
way he should go, and
when he is old he will
not depart from it.
Proverbs 22:6

About the Author

Shelley Vieira is a wife, mother, and grandmother (aka Vivi). She Is a resident of both the Central Valley and Central Coast of California. She is the author of *Kingdom Kids*, a book that teaches children to treasure the truth through rhymes and songs. Her desire is to lead both young and old to a childlike faith, so they remember how dearly the Father loves and cares for them. She loves to write and purposely places the Living Word of God within the pages she writes. She hopes that the Lord continues to give a sweet tune to accompany all her books because the Lord has been good to her, and therefore, she can't help but sing (Psalm 13:6).

About the Illustrator

Maggui Ledbetter graduated from CSU Fresno with a bachelor's degree and a teaching credential. After teaching for Los Banos Unified School District for thirty years, Maggui retired and now spends her days painting at home in her art studio. She enjoys painting with watercolors and acrylics and has a passion for using art to express the farmer's struggles with water shortages and politics and their love of farming. Maggui has illustrated for books such as *How Far is Heaven, Blanket of Miracles, Tulip's Journey*, and her own authored book entitled *The Pink Can Notes*. Maggui looks forward to more years of writing and painting.

If you would like to begin a personal relationship with
Jesus today, please pray this prayer:

Lord Jesus, I invite You into my life,
I believe You died for me and that Your blood pays
for my sins and provides me with the gift of eternal life;
By faith I receive that gift and thank You for the Holy Spirit
that will now help me in this life.
I accept You as my Lord and Savior. Amen.

CPSIA information can be obtained
at www.ICGtesting.com
Printed in the USA
BVRC092200220721
612366BV00001B/3